This
Awakening
Generation

Lakewood Church
P.O. Box 23297
Houston, TX 77228

Copyright © 1964 John Osteen

ISBN 0-912631-15-5

Contents

With tear-stained faces, these awakened people are climbing the hill of God to get above the fog and smog of tradition and sectarianism. They want more than religion. They don't want to be proselyted into another denomination. They don't want to be fitted into another doctrinal mold so that someone may gloat over them as converts. They want something greater than all denominational groups.

These seeking hearts want God and the power of His Holy Spirit. They want the miracle life of the Lord Jesus Christ that comes through the mighty baptism in the Holy Ghost. They want God's supernatural, miracle-working power—power that will enable them to effectively reach lost, doomed, and dying souls before it is everlastingly too late.

CHAPTER 1

This Awakening Generation

Like a sleeping giant rousing itself out of a deep sleep, the true Church, which is the body of Christ, is awakening.

Through the Prophet Joel, God said, *And it shall come to pass...that I will pour out my spirit upon all flesh* (Joel 2:28). This prophecy is being fulfilled today.

Ministers and members of all the historic denominations are receiving the baptism in the Holy Ghost. They are speaking in other tongues, praying for the sick, casting out devils, seeing miracles, and experiencing the mighty gifts of the Spirit as recorded in 1 Corinthians, chapter 12, and demonstrated in the Book of Acts.

Testimonies from men and women from all walks of life who have received this enduement of power are stirring the denominational world. Medical doctors, lawyers, scientists, ambassadors, nationally recognized industrialists, and folks from ordinary walks of life are telling of the supernatural power of God that has come to their lives since receiving the baptism in the Holy Ghost. In some states, almost every minister in certain historic non-Pentecostal denominations has received this experience.

This great outpouring has caught the attention of the press. National magazines, newspapers, and religious periodicals are reporting this mighty move of God.

The world renowned evangelist, Billy Graham, speaking to the Full Gospel Business Men's Convention in Seattle, Washington, said, "I find all over the country and through the world little prayer groups springing up everywhere. They are not organized and I pray God they never will be organized. They are unrelated to one another. People that ten years ago would have made fun of you are now engaged in the same type of meetings that you (Full Gospel people) are engaged in. We believe this is a move of the Spirit of God! It doesn't make headlines but, down underneath, *something is happening* and I believe it is God."

Something is happening!

The Lord said, *When the enemy shall come in like a flood, the Spirit of the Lord shall lift up a standard against him* (Isaiah 59:19). The enemy has certainly come in like a flood! The distress of nations is alarming. The restlessness of the masses is frightening. And men's hearts are failing them for fear of the things coming upon the earth (see Luke 21:26).

A spirit of Godlessness is sliding like a serpent across the world, sending its deadly venom into the lives of countless millions of people. Satan has joined the world with the church. The church is so worldly and the world is so "churchy" that it is difficult to tell the difference between the two.

6

In the midst of all this, God has begun to move. The Spirit of the Lord is settling like a mantle upon those who are hungry for more of God. This awakening comes from God and is raising up a standard against the enemy.

In my own experience as an ordained Southern Baptist minister, I found it so. After college and seminary training, I settled down to fulfill my calling the best way I knew. After nineteen years in the ministry, I suddenly began to search and seek after the deeper things of God.

My receiving the baptism in the Holy Ghost was not the result of Pentecostal indoctrination. No one came to convince me that I should seek this experience. On the contrary! The blessed Holy Spirit moved quietly but deeply in my soul. His presence created such a hunger for the supernatural that I sought out full gospel believers to help me find the power of God.

At the time, I felt that this was simply God's way of dealing with me as an individual. But, to my utter amazement, I discovered that this was happening all over the world.

In our offices in Houston, Texas, letters come from people around the globe who have heard of this experience. From England, Canada, France, Germany, Australia, South America, India, and other parts of the world, they write with great joy, telling of this outpouring of the Holy Spirit in their lives also. These are ministers and members of the historic denominations. Glory to God for His merciful visitation to His people everywhere!

This is a new day!

There was a time when those in the denominational churches would turn a deaf ear to the message of the supernatural power of God as revealed in the Book of Acts, but that is not so today. Never, in all the history of denominationalism, have people's hearts been more open and receptive to the message of the miracle-working power of the Lord Jesus Christ than they are today. People are tired of a "denominationalized" Jesus who seems to have lost His supernatural power to heal the sick, deliver those who are demon possessed, and perform miracles. They are sick and tired of being sick and tired. They are weary of a form of godliness that denies the power thereof (see 2 Timothy 3:5). Their hearts are stirred with new desire for more of God's power. As quiet desperation grips their hearts in this dark hour, they are turning their faces to God, seeking the answer—and they will not be denied!

Sincere and seeking hearts are awakening to the fact that Pentecost is not a denomination but an experience from God that is available to everyone. They are beginning to realize that traditions of men have robbed them of their rightful heritage as sons and daughters of God. Because of their awakening, they know that Jesus Christ is, indeed, *the same yesterday, and to day, and for ever* (Hebrews 13:8).

With tear-stained faces, these awakened people are climbing the hill of God to get above the fog and smog of tradition and sectarianism. They want more than religion. They don't want to be proselyted into another denomination. They don't want to be fitted into another doctrinal mold so that someone may gloat over them as converts. They want something greater than all denominational groups.

These seeking hearts want God and the power of His Holy Spirit. They want the miracle life of the Lord Jesus Christ that comes through the mighty baptism in the Holy Ghost. They want God's supernatural, miracle-working power—power that will enable them to effectively reach lost, doomed, and dying souls before it is everlastingly too late.

In every denomination...in every nation...on every continent, God is responding swiftly to hungry and searching hearts—clothing them with His power and sending them forth to tell the world of Jesus, who died to set men free.

Tradition is crumbling before the Word of God. It is melting like a fog before the rising sun. The walls of tradition are not high enough or strong enough to hold the desperate, hungry people in this dark hour of human history. They are hearing the sound of a distant drummer calling to them to march in tune with the Word of God instead of the teaching of man.

Praise God, there has arisen a generation that dares to believe God! You are a part of that generation and shall have your share of God's power to enable you to fulfill His perfect will in your life!

CHAPTER 2

I Was Among the Captives

*Now it came to pass in the thirtieth year, in the fourth month, in the fifth day of the month, as **I was among the captives** by the river of Chebar, that the heavens were opened, and I saw visions of God* (Ezekiel 1:1).

After nineteen years of preaching sincerely about the Lord Jesus Christ, I was awakened to the fact that I, too, was among the captives.

No, I wasn't a captive of Satan, like a lost man. I had no doubts about my salvation. In 1939, I walked down a church aisle in Fort Worth, Texas, and gave my heart to the Lord Jesus Christ. I was washed in His precious blood and experienced the new birth. Old things passed away and behold, all things became new (see 2 Corinthians 5:17). But, still, I was a captive.

In spite of the fact that I preached, witnessed, built churches, conducted revivals, and wept and prayed, I was still a captive.

In 1958, I left my library, taking only one powerful book—the Bible. I went away to be alone and set my face toward God. During this time alone with God and the Bible, I was awakened to the realization that I was, indeed, a captive. Jesus said, *Ye make the commandment of God of none effect by your tradition* (Matthew 15:6).

I was a captive of TRADITION—the teaching of man!

During my many years as a minister, I had read, again and again, the Word of God, but many of its commandments were ineffective in my life because of my traditions.

God clearly states His plan for us in the Bible, but many times we cannot see it because of the traditions of men. Hebrews 13:8 declares, *Jesus Christ the same yesterday, and to day, and for ever.* But tradition said He had changed—that He no longer would heal the sick, cast out demons, and deliver mankind from the powers of darkness. Tradition said He was no longer moved with such compassion for the needs of the multitudes that He healed them all. Tradition said **yesterday** He cared for mankind—body, soul, and spirit. But **today** He saves the soul and leaves the body to be ravaged by demons and disease.

The commandment of God was made of none effect by the tradition of man. I was a captive of that tradition!

I knew from the Gospels that Jesus was a compassionate, healing, powerful, delivering Savior. I followed Him through the pages of the Bible and rejoiced as He opened the eyes of the blind, caused the deaf to hear and the dumb to speak. I was thrilled as He cast out demons, raised the dead, and sent the multitudes home, healed by His power. How my heart burned within me as I read about the matchless Son of God ministering to the human race. But my tradition said He no longer did these things.

What about healing today?

My tradition said that our nervous, upset, distraught, demon-oppressed, sick and dying generation would have to get along with a Jesus who had left His supernatural power and compassion in the grave.

Tradition said that Jesus would no longer do what He did in the Bible. He cared for the blind of the Bible but not for the blind of today. He cared for the demon possessed in the Bible but not the demon possessed of today. He healed the deaf, dumb, crippled, paralyzed and diseased in the Bible, but He would not heal those who lived today.

I was a captive of that tradition!

But God plainly states in His Word that He is able—and willing—to heal the sick. It is abundantly clear that He wants the ministry of healing to be operating in His church—today.

The very first promise God gave to a redeemed people was, *I am* [Jehovah Rapha] *the Lord that healeth thee* (Exodus 15:26). Isaiah declared, "He was made sick with our sicknesses, and with His stripes we are healed" (see Isaiah 53:4,5). And the thrilling message David sang in Psalm 103:1-3 is, *Bless the Lord, O my soul: and all that is within me, bless his holy name. Bless the Lord, O my soul, and forget not all his benefits: Who forgiveth all thine iniquities; who healeth all thy diseases.*

Jesus spent the greatest portion of His ministry healing the sick. I used to sing a little chorus, "To be like Jesus, to be like Jesus. All I ask is to

13

be like Him." But I didn't realize it was absolutely impossible to be like Jesus without praying for the sick. For Jesus commanded the twelve disciples to heal the sick (see Matthew 10:1,8). He commanded the seventy to heal the sick (see Luke 10:1,8,9). And He commands ALL BELIEVERS to minister to the sick as they take the Gospel to every creature (see Mark 16:15-18).

James 5:14 says, *Is any sick among you? let him call for the elders of the church....* They were instructed to pray over him, anointing him with oil in the name of Jesus. The promise was that the prayer of faith would save him and the Lord would raise him up.

The works of Jesus...and the Church

The Book of Acts is a clear picture of what the Lord wants His church to do—it is to go forth with signs and miracles in the name of Jesus through the power of the Holy Ghost. Jesus said, *He that believeth on me, the works that I do shall he do also; and greater works than these shall he do; because I go unto my Father* (John 14:12).

Tradition, however, rose like a giant to contradict all of this. When Jesus said, "The works that I do shall ye do also," tradition said, "The works of Jesus ye shall *not* do."

The Bible said plainly, *They shall lay hands on the sick, and they shall recover* (Mark 16:18). But tradition said, "You shall *not* lay hands on the sick and they shall *not* recover."

Tradition and the teaching of man warned us, again and again, to stay away from those who

14

prayed for the sick and cast out demons, for they were "false prophets with lying signs and wonders."

The commandment of God was made of none effect by the tradition of man. I was a captive of these traditions.

The Holy Spirit—a separate experience

God's Word teaches that all of His children need the power of the Holy Spirit. *Not by might, nor by power, but by my spirit, saith the Lord* (Zechariah 4:6).

It is also abundantly clear that the enduement of power through the baptism in the Holy Ghost is a separate experience from salvation. Jesus was born of the Spirit, but that was not enough for Him. He never performed a miracle nor did anything about delivering mankind until He received a special enduement of power at His baptism in water. It was there that the Holy Ghost came upon Him in the form of a dove. From that time on, He was well-known for the miraculous wonders He performed.

The disciples were saved before Pentecost. Jesus said to them, *Rejoice not, that the spirits are subject unto you; but rather rejoice, because your names are written in heaven* (Luke 10:20). This was not enough, however. They still needed power. *And, being assembled together with them, [Jesus] commanded them that they should not depart from Jerusalem, but wait for the promise of the Father, which, saith he, ye have heard of me.*

For John truly baptized with water; but ye shall be baptized with the Holy Ghost not many days hence (Acts 1:4,5). Jesus said, in effect, "Don't you dare go to this hell-bound, demon-possessed, devil-oppressed, darkened, dying world until you are clothed with the power of the Holy Ghost.

In Luke 11:13, Jesus said, *If ye then, being evil, know how to give good gifts unto your children: how much more shall your heavenly Father give the Holy Spirit to them that ask him?*

Sinners who come to repent and accept Jesus as Savior don't ask for the Holy Spirit. They ask for forgiveness and eternal life through the Lord Jesus. *God's gift to the sinner is eternal life.*

But when the sinner is cleansed in the blood and made acceptable in the Beloved, he should ask for the Holy Spirit, for *God's gift to the believer is the Holy Spirit.*

Paul was saved on the road to Damascus, but it was three days later that he was healed and filled with the Spirit (see Acts 9).

Salvation and receiving the Holy Spirit are two separate experiences. God makes this very clear in Acts 8:5-7,12,14-15, *Then Philip went down to the city of Samaria, and preached Christ unto them. And the people with one accord gave heed unto those things which Philip spake, hearing and seeing the miracles which he did. For unclean spirits, crying with loud voice, came out of many that were possessed with them: and many taken with palsies, and that were lame, were healed...But when they believed Philip preaching the things concerning the kingdom of God, and the name of*

Jesus Christ, they were baptized, both men and women...Now when the apostles which were at Jerusalem heard that Samaria had received the word of God, they sent unto them Peter and John: who, when they were come down, prayed for them, that they might receive the Holy Ghost. These saved people, who had been baptized in water, received the Holy Ghost through a separate experience.

In the face of these great truths, tradition cried out, "We received all that was necessary when we accepted Jesus as Savior. There is no need to tarry for another experience of power, for we have it all!"

Speaking in tongues

Tradition is the avowed arch enemy of the manifestation of the Spirit known as "speaking in tongues." I was a captive of this tradition.

One of the last messages Jesus gave to His church is found in Mark 16:17, where He said, *These signs shall follow them that believe.* The verse goes on to list the signs. One of the signs is, *In my name...they shall speak with new tongues.*

Acts 2:4 says, *They were all filled with the Holy Ghost, and began to speak with other tongues, as the Spirit gave them utterance.*

Ten years later, when Peter preached to the house of Cornelius, they all spoke in tongues (see Acts 10).

Twenty years after Pentecost, Paul laid his hands upon the elders of Ephesus and they all spake in tongues and prophesied (see Acts 19).

17

Paul said, *I speak with tongues more than ye all* (1 Corinthians 14:18), and *Forbid not to speak with tongues* (1 Corinthians 14:39). He declared through the Spirit that he who speaks in tongues edifies himself, edifies the Church, magnifies God, and is a sign to the unbeliever (see 1 Corinthians 14).

~~Stop~~ The tradition of man roars in anger, "I forbid you to speak in tongues! Speaking in tongues is a sign of over-emotionalism and fanaticism! People who speak in tongues are full of the devil! They magnify themselves. It does no good. Speaking in tongues ceased with the apostles." I was a captive of this tradition.

Paul said, *Though we, or an angel from heaven, preach any other gospel unto you than that which we have preached unto you, let him be accursed* (Galatians 1:8). Follow Paul in his ministry and listen to him preach and you will know what kind of Gospel he had. He said, *My speech and my preaching was not with enticing words of man's wisdom, but in demonstration of the Spirit and of power* (1 Corinthians 2:4). Paul preached a Gospel that he could demonstrate. He healed the sick, cast out demons, and saw believers baptized in the Holy Ghost and fire. Thousands were saved and delivered through this supernatural Gospel.

I was awakened to the fact that, in that dark hour of human history, when the supernatural was needed as never before, I was preaching "another gospel"—one that took its stand against the very things the true Gospel proclaimed.

18

The truth will make you free

John 8:32 says, *Ye shall know the truth, and the truth shall make you free.* It was the Word of God that set me free! I found God's pattern for His church in the Book of Acts. It is a Church that believes in salvation by grace, the baptism in the Holy Ghost and fire, speaking in tongues, prophecy, visions, revelations, healings, miracles, and the gifts of the Spirit. His people are to be clothed with power to bring the message of salvation in its fullest sense to every creature.

Yes, like Ezekiel, I was among the captives. But, praise God, the heavens opened and I saw visions of God. The chains snapped, and this captive was set free!

I was free to march forth to a lost world as they did in the Book of Acts—free to have the power they had to do the things they did!

Jesus said in Luke 4:18, *The Spirit of the Lord is upon me, because he hath anointed me to preach the gospel to the poor; he hath sent me to heal the brokenhearted, to preach deliverance to the captives, and recovering of sight to the blind, to set at liberty them that are bruised.*

Thank God, He set this captive free! And what I have experienced is also occurring in the lives of countless thousands of others around the world.

Tradition is crumbling before the Word of God. It is melting like a fog before the rising sun. The walls of tradition are not high enough or strong enough to hold the desperate, hungry people in this dark hour of human history. They are hearing the sound of a distant drummer calling to them to march in tune with the Word of God instead of the teaching of man.

Praise God, there has arisen a generation that dares to believe God! You are a part of that generation and shall have your share of God's power to enable you to fulfill His perfect will in your life!

In that air-conditioned room, with my hands lifted up to heaven and my heart reaching out for my God, there came the glory of His power. It poured in like a stream from heaven. I spoke in another language. The same Spirit that hovered over the world in the beginning now rested on me. The same Spirit that anointed Jesus with miraculous power was now in me, to enable me to do His works...and even greater works, because He had gone to the Father. I went forth from that place with the mantle of His power and set my face toward a world that desperately needed Jesus.

CHAPTER 3

Clothed With Power

But tarry ye in the city of Jerusalem, until ye be endued [clothed] *with power from on high* (Luke 24:49).

This chapter is the story of a man's search after God's power. It is the story of a man in the deep, dark hole of tradition, chained and shackled by the teachings of man.

Teachings of man

I was taught that having the Holy Ghost and power in this day was a lie. I ridiculed it. I just didn't think it was real. I believed as I was taught—that the day of miracles was past, tongues and prophecy had ceased, and praying for the sick was useless because that day was gone forever. I felt that casting out demons was a sign of ignorance.

In spite of what the Bible clearly said, I was convinced that a person received all that he would ever get from God when he was saved and washed in the blood of Jesus Christ. I was really saved in Fort Worth, Texas, in 1939, when I repented of my sins and gave my heart to Jesus. I felt the call to preach, so I began to prepare myself. After graduation from college and seminary, I pastored Baptist churches for many, many years. I was the assistant pastor at First Baptist Church of San

Diego, California, for some time. I was pastor of First Baptist Church of Hamlin, Texas, for approximately three years. I was an evangelist for two years, holding revivals in many Southern Baptist churches. Then I pastored Central Baptist Church in Baytown, Texas (near Houston), for six and a half years. I pastored Hibbard Memorial Baptist Church in Houston, Texas, for three years. I also pastored Lakewood Baptist Church of Houston, Texas.

I cried and prayed over my sermons. I conducted revivals and saw many people saved. My desire was to be completely dedicated to God. Just because a preacher or church member doesn't understand the baptism in the Holy Ghost doesn't mean that he does not love Jesus and serve Him in sincerity. Thousands of preachers and their members do not fully understand the baptism in the Holy Ghost, but they are saved and they love the Lord. They are acting in all the light they have. They are products of this generation and its teachings.

It was said of Cornelius and his household, *The Holy Ghost fell on all them which heard the word* (Acts 10:44). Many today have not heard the Word concerning these things. It is our responsibility to present what the Word of God teaches about the experience so they will believe.

Something is missing

I write as a representative of the professional ministry of our day. I use this term in the highest sense, not meaning a minister who feels no divine call. I am only one of many preachers of our day who is desperately concerned and deeply disturbed about the lack of power in the ministry today. As a Christian and minister, I knew the Spirit of God had regenerated me, and yet there was something missing in my life. There was a growing concern in my heart—I needed something more.

I preached about praying, but deep in my heart I didn't really love to pray consistently. I preached about loving God's Word, but my congregation would have been amazed to know how little time I spent reading it. I preached about the presence, power, and blessing of God, but when I faced the facts, I didn't have an abundance of them in my life. Oh, how many preachers cry out in their hearts for a greater manifestation of these things in their lives. We can pray, love and read the Word, and feel the blessing for a short time ...then it's back in the valley.

My members streamed down the aisles, weeping and seeking more power from God, but what could I say? Oh, my soul cried out! A lost and dying, wicked, perverse world needed help. But I needed more power to enable me to give that help. My members would say, "Oh, Pastor, I want more power to live for Jesus. Can you tell me how to find it?" I would just say, "I'll pray for you." They were unaware that, in the secret places of my heart, I, too, longed and prayed for that same power.

Detour through the business world

My heart grew heavier and heavier as the

years went by. I remember sitting in my study in Baytown, Texas. I read the Book of Acts and marveled at the miraculous and supernatural power of God in the lives of those early Christians. My heart cried out, "Oh, God, I wish it could happen today!" But every bit of my training rose up to say, "It's not for today." I heard the voices of my professors in college and seminary saying, "It's not for today." Every book in my library said, "It can't happen today." So I closed my Bible and went wearily about the task of pastoring about a thousand people who were members of my church.

This is the condition of thousands of people today. It ought to make us weep. It ought to make us cry, "Gabriel, put the flag of heaven at half-mast and sound the saddest note on your trumpet. In the darkest hour of human history, when we ought to be clothed with power, we are in the valley of despair!"

Finally, in desperation, I decided to leave my church and enter the business world. I said, "I'll not be a hypocrite. My soul cries out for a more satisfying experience with God and I cannot seem to find it. It seems I cannot pull back the curtains. I cannot understand, so I'll just quit pastoring and enter the business world."

No, I didn't turn my back on the Lord Jesus Christ. I didn't turn my back on the ministry and call of God. Because I was confused, disturbed, and discontented I decided I was through pastoring churches. I decided to enter the business world and make money. I planned to preach on weekends, or whenever I was needed, in various churches—and this I did. I plunged myself deep into making money. I never intended to pastor another church as long as I lived.

I was startled by something I discovered out in the business world. Many people were not even aware that I was a Christian, much less that I was a minister. I met all kinds of people as I engaged in business. I was astounded and amazed to find that many professing Christians (some who held prominent places in church organizations) used profanity, drank liquor, told dirty stories, and seemingly had no spirituality at all. They were religious but not spiritual. I was amazed to see Sunday school teachers holding cocktail glasses and to hear them using profanity.

I was in the office of a man who was using quite a bit of profanity in conversation. I brought up the name of Jesus and started talking to him about his need for God. This man was puzzled. He pointed to a large book on his desk and informed me that he was the leader and teacher of a deeper life course in his local church.

One day another man called me on the telephone. In just five minutes, I heard the most filthy, obscene language I had ever heard in my life. When he finished talking, I felt so unclean that I wanted to take a bath. But that was just his normal way of talking. Just a few hours later, this same man was at a dinner meeting I attended at a hotel in Houston, Texas. They called on him to pray. If I had not heard his conversation a few hours earlier, I would have thought he was the best Christian in Houston. He prayed a very fundamental, evangelical prayer and concluded by saying, "I ask this in the Name of our Lord and Savior, Jesus Christ."

When I heard this man pray, I said, "My God! My God! What have we come to? In the darkest hour of human history, is this what has been produced in the name of Christianity?" It startled my soul. I was alarmed down in the deepest part of my being. I said, "Do these people think they are going to heaven? Do they think they are right with God? Do they think they have the power to face the Godlessness of this generation and the supernatural march of the devil in this hour?"

I realized that somebody had to do something about the situation. God pointed His finger at me and said, "Well, what have you done? You haven't paid the price to seek My face and find My power." God spoke again, "This is the product of the 'easy-believism' that you have been preaching."

Oh, my dear friends, you have to do more than say, "I believe in Jesus Christ," to be saved. You must sincerely repent and accept Him as your personal Savior. You must be washed in His blood and be born again. You must have more than religion. You must have eternal life through Jesus Christ!

I made a decision and said, "If no one else does anything about this situation, here is one man who will." I determined to set my face toward God and try again. Oh, thank God, for the sweet Holy Ghost, who never loses a battle!

Search for power

As a result of these experiences, I decided to accept the pastorate of Hibbard Memorial Baptist Church in Houston, Texas. I set my face to seek God with all my heart. I said, "I know there is a God in heaven. The Bible is His Word and His Son is Jesus Christ, the One who saved my soul. I am going to find more power, and I am going to find that power for the sake of my generation."

I was weary of a form of godliness that denied the power thereof. I was in the deep, dark hole of tradition, chained by the teaching of man. But somewhere, I knew there was light. Somewhere, I knew there was victory. Somewhere, I knew there was freedom. And I set my soul to find that freedom so I could be free from the chains of sectarianism and the tradition of man.

Along with a group of men in my church, I began to seek God. We met early every Sunday morning and at other times through the week, and cried, prayed, sought, and pleaded for the power of God.

This may surprise you, but not once, during this time of agonizing and searching for God's power, did it ever cross my mind that I might need the baptism of the Holy Ghost or a Pentecostal experience. In all my time of pleading with God, not once did it cross my mind that I might get mixed up with the fanatics who speak in tongues, prophesy, pray for the sick, and cast out devils. I felt that those things were only for days gone by. I felt that we could have the power of God to make us great preachers or give us a place of prominence, but surely the power of God would not do today what it did for the people in the Bible.

Do you know the tragedy of this preacher's heart and life? God was trying to lead me into the baptism of the Holy Ghost, and I didn't even know it. Tragedy of tragedies! It's enough to make the angels weep! Like many others, I was saved, called and prepared for the professional ministry, and still didn't recognize that God was seeking to lead me into the baptism of the Holy Ghost and fire.

Oh, the preachers of our day have God's hand upon them, but they do not recognize that God is seeking to baptize them in the Holy Ghost and fire! This was one reason I left the pastorate for a time and launched out as an evangelist to go across the land and around the world to be a blessing and help to these hungry-hearted preachers. Quiet desperation grips their very souls. The irrepressible call of God is upon them, and the hour is too late for them to fail God. They are setting their faces toward the Lord as never before. They know that they are called to be more than a denominational servant. The fire of a prophet burns within them. They want God's power but, like this preacher, many of them do not recognize that God is seeking to lead them into the full baptism in the Holy Ghost and fire.

As I look back upon my life and think about how I was trapped in this dark hole of tradition, I realize that I never would have gotten out in my own strength. You say, "Brother Osteen, you could have believed if you had wanted to believe." That is easier said than done. After being trained in school against these things, and after preaching for many years that they are not so, you cannot snap your fingers and automatically change. Do you know what brought me out of this dark hole of tradition? Do you know what snapped the chains and set this captive free? It was the supernatural power of God. I cannot emphasize it enough. It is the supernatural power of God that sets men free!

Baby girl brings joy...and concern

About this time, our little girl was born. When she arrived, we were filled with joy. But soon that joy turned to great concern. We noticed that she could not move normally. The doctor was concerned and had her x-rayed. They could find no broken bones, so they released her and we took her home. After several weeks, we took her to a specialist in the Houston area. After examining our child, the specialist turned to my wife and said, "Mrs. Osteen, your child is not normal. She has had a birth injury and will either be spastic or have something of that nature. She definitely is not normal."

Of course, anyone could see there was a problem. Her color was strange. She had no muscle tone and was unable to move properly. In fact, our baby never did crawl. She never had strength enough to crawl. She only scooted across the floor.

This was, indeed, a dark hour in our lives.

As I looked at our little baby girl and thought about the fact that she would never live a normal life, strange emotions came into my heart. I had always been taught to shun the idea of praying for the sick. Divine healers and healing services were things a professional preacher dared not touch or he might lose his prestige and good standing. But when it's your child, it's different—you want to **know** what God has promised. And I was determined to find out.

My search for truth

As I looked at our little baby, I said in my heart, "I don't care what college and seminary professors taught me. And I don't care what dark tradition says. I am going to take the Word of God and I am going to find out what God has to say to us about our baby."

John 8:32 says, *You shall know the truth, and the truth shall make you free.* As I earnestly sought the truth in God's Word, I was amazed to discover that it was not God who made people sick, but it was the devil. God revealed himself as a Healer. God revealed through Jesus Christ that it was His desire to heal the sick. He said, *The thief cometh not, but for to steal, and to kill, and to destroy: I am come that they might have life, and that they might have it more abundantly* (John 10:10).

Because the devil deceived Adam and Eve, sickness and death were brought into the world. It was the devil who caused Job to be smitten with sore boils. It was the devil who made people sick! And it was the Lord Jesus who healed them! Acts 10:38 says, *God anointed Jesus of Nazareth with the Holy Ghost and with power: who went about doing good, and healing all that were oppressed of the devil.* He didn't heal people who had been oppressed of the Father. He healed those who had been oppressed of the devil! He didn't heal people whose sicknesses came from the Father. He healed those whose sicknesses came from the devil! Every sickness was brought on by the devil, but praise God, Jesus healed them all!

Jesus—the Healer

I was astounded to discover that the first promise God gave to a redeemed people was, *I am the Lord that healeth thee* (Exodus 15:26). Isn't that wonderful?

As I went on through the Bible, I saw David pick up his harp and begin to sing, *Bless the Lord, O my soul, and forget not all his benefits: who forgiveth all thine iniquities; who healeth all thy diseases* (Psalm 103:2,3). I heard the prophet say, *But unto you that fear my name shall the Sun of righteousness arise with healing in his wings* (Malachi 4:2). I heard Isaiah say, "He was made sick with our sicknesses and with his stripes we are healed" (see Isaiah 53:4,5).

As I came to the Gospels, I said, "Lord Jesus, I have preached about You for nineteen years. Let me take Your hand and go through these pages again and see if You have anything to say to me in this dark hour." I took the hand of Jesus and walked with Him through Matthew, Mark, Luke, and John. I saw Him open the eyes of the blind and make the lame to walk, the deaf to hear, and the dumb to speak. I saw the miraculous life of Jesus Christ. I saw that He spent at least 75 percent of His time healing sick bodies and casting out demons. I said, "My God in heaven, could this be the same Jesus that I have preached for nineteen years? All He does is heal the sick, cast out devils, and deliver mankind."

Could He be the same Jesus? I hardly knew Him. Why, I knew more about the Apostle Paul than I did about Jesus Christ! Then the truth of Hebrews 13:8 came like thunder into my soul! *Jesus Christ the same yesterday, to day, and for ever.* He is the same. He has not changed! He is the same yesterday, today, and forever!

When I discovered this truth, there was never another doubt in my mind about the healing of our baby. I said, "If this Jesus is the same, He will heal her. If He has the same compassion and love, and the same power and desire to heal the sick as I see in the Bible, He will heal our baby." I read the command and promise in James 5:14,15, *Is any sick among you? let him call for the elders of the church; and let them pray over him, anointing him with oil in the name of the Lord: and the prayer of faith shall save the sick, and the Lord shall raise him up.*

I read the Great Commission in Mark 16, *These signs shall follow them that believe; In my name...they shall lay hands on the sick, and they shall recover* (vs. 17,18).

We decided to believe God and His Word. We anointed our baby with oil. We laid our hands on her and prayed for her in the Name of the Lord Jesus Christ. We took our stand upon the Word of God. Daily, we praised God for His Word and the promises in His Word.

When we took our baby back to the specialist after a few weeks, he declared that she was absolutely normal! She is perfectly normal today—a college graduate and a vital part of our ministry. Why? Because Jesus Christ is the same yesterday, today, and forever!

A breakthrough

When this happened, I found myself rising out of the deep dark hole of tradition. I felt some of the chains snap and fall from my spirit. I could see light at the top of this dark hole of tradition, and I knew that there was more than I had been taught to believe. But even though I could see light, I was not out of that dark hole. Something else needed to happen to make me believe for the supernatural power of God.

I knew a man who had the baptism in the Holy Ghost, and I was never very comfortable around him because He was always praising God. That made me very nervous and irritated—I didn't like that, but I liked him. I knew that one day he would try to convince me that his form of religion and worship was better than mine, so I was always on guard when I was in his company.

One day as we ate lunch together, he said, "You know, Brother Osteen, a wonderful thing happened in one of our church services recently. A teenage girl got lost in the Spirit of God." I thought to myself that I knew all about that fanaticism and I wasn't interested in such things. But I listened just to be polite. He continued, "She began to speak in another language." I thought, "Yes, and she'll soon be in an institution. This is over-emotionalism and fanaticism." I didn't want anything to do with it, so I shut my mind and plugged up my ears. But he continued, "A missionary in the congregation, just returned from Africa, jumped to his feet and said to the congregation, 'This child is speaking in the language of the tribe that I ministered to in Africa. She is praising and worshipping the Lord in that tribal language.'"

My friend didn't realize it, but a bomb exploded in my soul. He didn't ask me to believe it or disbelieve it—He simply stated it as a fact. I said to myself, "Great God in heaven, could there be any reality to this that I have turned my back on and ignored?"

This was the first time that I had come face to face with the supernatural gift of tongues and the gift of interpretation of tongues. And the very first time I faced it, I believed it. No words can describe what went on in my heart and life as this supernatural manifestation of the Holy Ghost was presented to me. Every chain snapped from my soul, and I was hurled out of the dark hole of tradition!

I realized, as I faced the supernatural gifts of God in tongues and interpretation, that these things were happening today. I realized the Bible had said what it meant and meant what it said. I was free to take the Word of God and believe it! I closed my library once again, for I was determined to have only the Bible. I had listened to man, tradition, and denominations long enough. In this dark hour, I was going to find out what God had to say.

Searching the Word

I studied my Bible alone in my office in downtown Houston. I was there day and night. During one of those days, the wonderful revelation came. I read of Moses, Elijah, Elisha, Jesus, the Early Church, and the disciples. I read carefully the commands and desires of our Lord Jesus Christ. I began to see that we are sent to help a darkened, hell-bound, demon-ridden world—but we are not to do it in our own power. It was God's plan that His people have a supernatural ministry. It was, and still is, His plan for us to have His power today, in this twentieth century. God's plan is for His supernatural power to destroy the works of the devil and set men free!

Oh, how well I remember when this revelation came to me and I knew that it was true! I wept before the Lord. As I drove the sixteen miles to my home, I shouted and praised the God of the miraculous! "My God, it is true! My God, it is true! No wonder I have been confused and defeated. Praise the Lord!" God had revealed His way to my soul.

As a result of this experience, there was born

in me a burning desire to have the same ministry as the early disciples. Oh, how I wanted to see the sick healed by the supernatural power of God. How I wanted to see the Holy Ghost work miracles. I knew this was God's way and that it would awaken a sleeping world and bring to it the knowledge of Jesus and His love.

You see, when I set my heart to seek the baptism in the Holy Ghost, I was not seeking tongues—I was seeking power. I wanted a supernatural ministry. And to have that, I knew I had to have supernatural power.

Now, I am not ashamed that I speak in tongues—I am thrilled. Praise God for the benefits of speaking in tongues! I say with the Apostle Paul, *I would that ye all spake in tongues* (1 Corinthians 14:5). But, at that time, I only knew I was seeking supernatural power.

But Jesus said, *Ye shall receive power, after that the Holy Ghost is come upon you* (Acts 1:8). The early disciples had that power. I set my face to seek God that I, too, might have that power. With my traditional ears unplugged and the sectarian glasses off, how easy it was to see the truth in God's Word. I discovered that, even though Jesus was the Son of God, nothing was ever heard of His supernatural ministry on earth, until the Holy Ghost came upon Him. The Spirit drove Him into the wilderness, and when He came out, there went out a fame of Him throughout the land.

I found out that, even though the disciples were saved—with their names written in the Lamb's Book of Life—they didn't do much except argue and bicker over who was in first place until that blessed day in Acts, chapter 2. It was then, the Bible says, that *they were all filled with the Holy Ghost, and began to speak with other tongues, as the Spirit gave them utterance* (vs. 4).

In Acts, chapter 8, I found that Samaria had turned to God under the preaching of Philip. They believed on the Lord Jesus and were baptized in water. But Peter and John came from Jerusalem to pray that these saved people might receive the Holy Ghost.

As I went through the Bible, I read in Acts, chapter 10, about Cornelius, who had gathered together his relatives and friends to hear Peter. Verse 44 says, *While Peter yet spake...the Holy Ghost fell on all them which heard the word.*

I read in Acts 19:6, that as Paul laid his hands upon the elders at Ephesus, *the Holy Ghost came on them; and they spake with tongues, and prophesied.*

It was so clear from the Word of God that these saved people had *another* experience. It was called the baptism in the Holy Ghost. When they were clothed with this supernatural power, they invariably spoke in other tongues. This was a sign to them of His indwelling presence and mantle of power. And this was what I needed to reach my generation.

There followed weeks of waiting upon God—times of fasting and prayer and times of repentance and restitution. God let me sanctify and set myself apart to do His work in sincerity. In my deepest desperation for God's power, I told my wife that I was going away and would not return until I heard from heaven. I didn't expect to see her again for a month.

The Spirit rests on me!

I went to downtown Houston and rented a hotel room and shut myself up with God. I said, "Oh, God, the hour is too late, hell is too hot, heaven is too real, time is too short, eternity is too long, and my responsibility is too great for me to fail You in this hour. I want all heaven, all hell, and all creation to witness that I am willing to reach this generation by Your supernatural power."

The Lord said, "Are you willing to be numbered among the despised and those who are ostracized? Are you willing to lose the prestige of your denominational standing...to be fired from your church and have your salary cut off? Are you willing to have every door shut against you and never be invited to preach in their churches again? Are you willing to be ridiculed and embarrassed because people look upon you as a fanatic?"

To all of these questions, and many more, I cried, "I am! I am! I am!"

In that air-conditioned room, with my hands lifted up to heaven and my heart reaching out for my God, there came the glory of His power. It poured in like a stream from heaven. I spoke in another language for quite a long time. Glory to God!

The same Spirit that hovered over the world in the beginning now rested on me. The same Spirit that was upon Elijah, Elisha, and Moses now possessed me. I had the same Holy Ghost that Peter, Paul, and all the early disciples had. The same Spirit that anointed Jesus with miraculous power was now in me, to enable me to do His works...and even greater works, because He had gone to the Father. I went forth from that place with the mantle of His power, which would enable me to reach a lost and dying world. I could say with Jesus, *The Spirit of the Lord is upon me, because he hath anointed me to preach the gospel to the poor; he hath sent me to heal the broken-hearted, to preach deliverance to the captives, and recovering of sight to the blind, to set at liberty them that are bruised, to preach the acceptable year of the Lord* (Luke 4:18,19).

Note:

It was through the help of Brother and Sister J. R. Goodwin that I first spoke a few words in another language in their home in Pasadena, Texas. But only after waiting on God in that hotel room in downtown Houston did I receive the fullness of the experience of the baptism in the Holy Ghost.

I hear His stately footsteps! Oh, I hear the rustle of His garments! I feel the presence of His power! There is a noise in the valley...behold, there is a great shaking!

What is this noise? It is the noise of thousands of denominational people speaking in tongues...the noise of thousands of God's people prophesying, praying for the sick, and casting out devils.

What is this noise? It is the noise of the denominational people coming out of the chains of sectarianism and, in the mighty name of Jesus, claiming their rights, and setting captives free.

CHAPTER 4

A Noise in the Valley

The hand of the Lord was upon me, and carried me out in the spirit of the Lord, and set me down in the midst of the valley which was full of bones, and caused me to pass by them round about: and, behold, there were very many in the open valley; and, lo, they were very dry.

And he said unto me, Son of Man, can these bones live? And I answered, O Lord God, thou knowest. Again he said unto me, Prophesy upon these bones, and say unto them, O ye dry bones, hear the word of the Lord.

Thus saith the Lord God unto these bones; Behold, I will cause breath to enter into you, and ye shall live: And I will lay sinews upon you, and will bring up flesh upon you, and cover you with skin, and put breath in you, and ye shall live; and ye shall know that I am the Lord.

So I prophesied as I was commanded: and as I prophesied, there was a noise, and behold a shaking, and the bones came together, bone to his bone. And when I beheld, lo, the sinews and the flesh came up upon them, and the skin covered them above: but there was no breath in them.

Then said he unto me, Prophesy unto the wind, prophesy, son of man, and say to the wind, Thus saith the Lord God; Come from the four winds, O breath, and breathe upon these slain, *that they may live. So I prophesied as he commanded me, and the breath came into them, and they lived, and stood up upon their feet, an exceeding great army.*

Then he said unto me, Son of man, these bones are the whole house of Israel: behold, they say, Our bones are dried, and our hope is lost: we are cut off for our parts. Therefore prophesy and say unto them, Thus saith the Lord God; Behold, O my people, I will open your graves, and cause you to come up out of your graves, and bring you into the land of Israel.

And ye shall know that I am the Lord, when I have opened your graves, O my people, and brought you up out of your graves, and shall put my spirit in you, and ye shall live, and I shall place you in your own land: then shall ye know that I the Lord have spoken it, and performed it, saith the Lord (Ezekiel 37:1-14).

Israel had power

I want you to see Israel as she was in the beginning. She was a nation well acquainted with the supernatural power of God. Languishing under the heel of the great Egyptian dynasty, God had miraculously delivered her with signs and wonders and miracles. The entire nation of Egypt was shaken to its foundation by the supernatural power of God.

Israel was there when God, by His supernatural power, parted the Red Sea and they went over on dry land.

Israel was there when the Lord gave them the

pillar of fire by night and the cloud by day...and when the manna fell supernaturally upon the ground.

Israel was there when the bitter waters of Marah were made sweet by the power of God...and when the serpent's bite was causing death, they looked upon a brazen serpent on a pole, and lived.

Israel lived in the glorious supernatural and moved in the shadow of the Shekinah glory! Through supernatural power, she subdued kingdoms. The Israelites circled the city of Jericho and the walls fell down flat. Samson carried the gates of a city to a hill and he stayed there shouting the victory of God (see Judges 16:3). Nations trembled at the sight of God's glorious people who were surrounded by the supernatural power of God.

But notice how God pictures them in the Book of Ezekiel. As Ezekiel walked in the valley of dry bones, God said, "These gleaming, dry bones are the whole house of Israel. Their hope is gone. They are spiritually dead and in their graves."

Israel had lost the supernatural power! She was down in the valley of defeat and despair.

I am sure Ezekiel must have wept as he saw how God viewed His people. God said, "Can these bones live?" Ezekiel replied, "Lord, thou knowest." God said, "Ezekiel, prophesy." So up and down the valley Ezekiel prophesied. And the Bible says there was a noise in that valley...and a great shaking.

The Lord was once again moving upon His

people, giving them life! He filled them with His Spirit, and they stood—a mighty army—ready to do the will of Almighty God!

The Early Church

I want you to see the Church of the Living God as she was in the beginning. When I speak of the Church, I am speaking of the body of Christ. What kind of a church was it? What did they believe? What did they have in that first Church?

The true answers to these and many other questions are found in the Bible. The real revelation of God's church is found in the Book of Acts. It is an accurate and complete revelation of the kind of Church Jesus Christ started.

Acts, chapter 1, tells us that the Church was made up of people who were redeemed by His power, but who also had a command from the Lord Jesus Christ. Jesus said in Luke 24:49, *Tarry ye in the city of Jerusalem, until ye be endued with power from on high.* He said in Acts 1:5, *For John truly baptized with water; but ye shall be baptized with the Holy Ghost not many days hence.* This Church believed that salvation was by the grace of God, but it also believed that, after salvation, it needed to be endued with the power of the Holy Ghost. For Jesus said, *Ye shall receive power, after that the Holy Ghost is come upon you: and ye shall be witnesses unto me both in Jerusalem, and in all Judaea, and in Samaria, and unto the uttermost part of the earth* (Acts 1:8).

And when the day of Pentecost was fully come, they were all with one accord in one place. And suddenly there came a sound from heaven as of a rushing mighty wind, and it filled all the house where they were sitting. And there appeared unto them cloven tongues like as of fire, and it sat upon each of them. And they were all filled with the Holy Ghost, and began to speak with other tongues, as the Spirit gave them utterance (Acts 2:1-4). The church that Jesus started was a church that believed in speaking in tongues.

In Acts, chapter 3, Peter and John went to the temple to pray. When they met the crippled man, Peter said, *Silver and gold have I none; but such as I have give I thee: In the name of Jesus Christ of Nazareth rise up and walk* (vs. 6). This man arose, healed by the power of God, and thousands came to know Jesus as Savior. This church believed in miracles.

March on through the Book of Acts and you will find that this was a supernaturally-endowed church. They believed in salvation *and* the baptism in the Holy Ghost. They believed in tongues, prophecy, and the supernatural gifts of the Spirit. They believed in praying for the sick and casting out devils. They believed in the miraculous power of Almighty God. They had visions, revelations, and visitations. Jesus was ever-present with them to confirm His Divine and Holy Word by signs, miracles, and wonders.

When they were threatened, they prayed like this, *Lord, behold their threatenings: and grant unto thy servants, that with all boldness they may speak thy word, by stretching forth thine hand to heal; and that signs and wonders may be done by*

47

the name of thy holy child Jesus (Acts 4:29,30). No wonder the place was shaken!

They were not ashamed of speaking in tongues, prophesying, praying for the sick, and casting out devils. They were not ashamed of the miraculous and the supernatural. They had one consuming desire and that was to tell the world that Jesus Christ was indeed the Son of God...that He had arisen from the dead, and was alive to perform the same miracles in their day that He did before He was crucified! They went forth with signs, wonders, and miracles to convince a lost and dying world of their need for God. The powers of heathenism crumbled before them and thousands were gathered into the fold of God.

Muddy waters of tradition

The Church began as a mighty river of Holy Ghost-filled people. Like Ezekiel's river, which flowed from the temple, the Church brought life wherever it went. As one looks at that river today, however, he hardly recognizes it. For many centuries, various groups have poured their traditions and teachings into the river. Today, it is filled with so many doctrines and ideas that it leaves a person confused.

God never intended for this to happen—He didn't establish denominationalism. The Church, which is His body, is the important thing in this hour. But a great part of the Body today are professing believers who are ashamed of what was found in the Early Church. Oh, my friends, it is a sad picture indeed. The majority of those who profess faith in the Lord Jesus Christ are ashamed of the baptism in the Holy Ghost and fire, speaking in tongues, prophesying, praying for the sick, and casting out devils. Where is the supernatural, miraculous power of God today?

The Church today is like Samson of old. Samson had the supernatural power of God and did mighty exploits. He ripped the gates of a city off and carried them to the top of a hill. With the jawbone of an ass, he slew a thousand Philistines. But when Samson laid his head in the lap of Delilah, he lost his power. When his locks were shorn, he heard the cry, "The Philistines be upon thee! Samson, the Philistines be upon thee!" It was the crisis hour! And in that hour, he arose, shook himself, and wist not that the Lord had departed from him. His enemies came in and he had no supernatural power. So they bound him, blinded him, and put him at the mill to grind like a lowly beast of burden (see Judges 14,15,16). This is a picture of the modern Church.

Oh, yes, one day the Church had power! We can see that in the Book of Acts. Like Samson, she ripped the gates of heathenism apart! Through the mighty gifts of the Spirit, she brought deliverance to the captives! In the mighty name of Jesus, she cast out the demons of disease and oppression! The powers of darkness melted before her like the mist before the rising sun!

Yes, the Church had its great day, but the Church laid its head in the lap of tradition and the teaching of man. The Church listened to the lies of tradition for many centuries, and now she has been lulled to sleep by falsehoods which claim that the day of miracles is past. Tradition says that there is no need for the baptism in the Holy Ghost and power—that it is a shame and a disgrace to speak in tongues, prophesy, and cast out devils...it's too embarrassing. This kind of church has a form of godliness but denies the power thereof.

But in this hour, as desperation grips the hungry hearts of people around the world, they are not content with the teaching of man, but are determined to have what God has promised. These people are going "up river"—beyond the Baptist, Methodist, Lutheran, Catholic, Episcopalian, and every other denominational name. They are going back to the Book of Acts! They want to see this mighty Church before tradition muddied the waters! They know that the true picture of the Church is found in the Book of Acts. This Church is the body of Christ. Every individual who is born again, washed in the Blood of Jesus, and whose name is written in the Lamb's Book of Life is a member of this Church. Your denomination doesn't matter. If your name is written in the Lamb's Book of Life, you are a member of His body, which is the true Church.

The crisis hour is upon us!

The end of all things has come upon this generation. The threat of total annihilation is here! A spirit of Godlessness, like the great shadow of an oncoming storm, hovers over the entire world. The crisis hour is here!

The Church is seeking to shake itself and go out in power as it has in times past, only to find that it has no supernatural power! Tragedy of tragedies! Gabriel, sound the saddest note upon your trumpet and put the flag of heaven at half-mast! In the darkest hour of human history, when the Church needs the supernatural power of God more than ever, she is blinded by tradition, bound by man's teaching, and is grinding at the mill of religion without power.

But in this valley of dry bones, something is happening today! As in Ezekiel's day, so God is moving in our day. God was not content to leave Israel in the grave, as a valley of dry bones! He sent forth a man in the name of the Lord God to stand in the valley and to prophesy until there came a noise and a great shaking in that valley!

Once again, in our day, God has come to His people! This strange and wonderful move taking place across our land and around the world is a sign of His presence! I hear His stately footsteps! Oh, I hear the rustle of His garments! I feel the presence of His power! There is a noise in the valley...behold, there is a great shaking!

What is this noise? It is the noise of thousands of denominational people speaking in tongues...the noise of thousands of God's people prophesying, praying for the sick, and casting out devils.

What is this noise? It is the noise of the denominational people coming out of the chains of sectarianism and, in the mighty name of Jesus, claiming their rights, and setting captives free.

There is a noise in the valley! This noise is

catching the attention of the newspapers and magazines. It is circling the globe. All over the world, this noise of praise gives evidence that God's presence and power is coming back to His people!

And when the ark of the covenant of the Lord came into the camp, all Israel shouted with a great shout, so that the earth rang again. And when the Philistines heard the noise of the shout, they said, What meaneth the noise of this great shout in the camp of the Hebrews? And they understood that the ark of the Lord was come into the camp. And the Philistines were afraid, for they said, God is come into the camp. And they said, Woe unto us! (see 1 Samuel 4:5-7). The noise in the Church today is the ark and the glory of God's supernatural power returning again to His people.

God promised, *And it shall come to pass in the last days, saith God, I will pour out my Spirit upon all flesh: and your sons and your daughters shall prophesy, and your young men shall see visions, and your old men shall dream dreams. And on my servants and on my handmaidens I will pour out in those days of my Spirit; and they shall prophesy* (Acts 2:17,18).

As in the days of Moses, God is saying, "I have seen the affliction of my people. I have heard their cries, I know their sorrows, and I have come down to deliver them" (see Acts 7:34).

God's promise—*When the enemy shall come in like a flood, the Spirit of the Lord shall lift up a standard against him* (Isaiah 59:19)—is being fulfilled today! The enemy has surely come in like a flood, but the mantle of God's Holy Spirit power is falling around the world—**And, behold, there is a great shaking!**

Yes, entire denominations are being shaken today. Tradition is being shaken. Sectarianism and the teaching of man is being shaken today! This is God's hour to bring His people out of their graves and breathe His Holy Spirit into them. God does not look at the label we wear. He pays no attention to our denominational standing. God's eyes sweep over this world in search of hungry hearts. When He finds a hungry heart, He comes swiftly to fill it with His Holy Ghost power!

God declared, *And I will restore to you the years that the locust hath eaten, the cankerworm, and the caterpillar, and the palmerworm, my great army which I sent among you. And ye shall eat in plenty, and be satisfied, and praise the name of the Lord your God, that hath dealt wondrously with you: and my people shall never be ashamed* (Joel 2:25,26).

This is the day of God's great restoration! The Lord Jesus sees the end of the age approaching and He sees the waiting harvest of the heathen around the world. He is imparting His supernatural power so His people may go forth to a waiting harvest and gather it in before it is everlastingly too late.

If you do not have the mantle of the Holy Ghost power in your life, you probably know someone who is a burning bush in your strata of society.

Will you, like Moses, turn aside to investigate these burning bushes? If you will but turn aside from your prejudice, tradition, and denominational ideas and look into this glorious outpouring of the Holy Ghost, God will speak to you, also, and send you forth, clothed with signs and wonders.

CHAPTER 5

Burning Bushes

And, behold, the bush burned with fire, and...God called unto him out of the midst of the bush (Exodus 3:2,4).

Moses was one of God's men of deliverance. He was chosen and destined to lead the Children of Israel out of Egypt. As in the case of all of God's deliverers, his life was characterized by the supernatural.

When babies were being murdered all across the land, the life of baby Moses was supernaturally spared when Pharaoh's daughter felt compassion and kept him for her own.

God calls Moses

Moses felt a divine destiny for his life. In the deepest part of his being, something told him that he was created for a special work. He tried to do the will of God in his own strength, and, instead of being a deliverer for his people, he became a murderer. With fear and discouragement, he fled into the land of Midian.

Forty years passed with no word from God. Had Jehovah forgotten? Had He changed His mind? No doubt Moses felt that, at the age of eighty, he was now too old to do anything for God.

But the Eternal God declared in His Holy

Word, *For God's gifts and His call are irrevocable—He never withdraws them when once they are given, and He does not change His mind about those to whom He gives His grace or to whom He sends His call* (Romans 11:29, Amplified Version).

How did God reach this man on the back side of the desert? How was this failure, who had now grown old, thrust out to do a great work for God? God reached him through a burning bush.

Now Moses kept the flock of Jethro his father in law, the priest of Midian: and he led the flock to the backside of the desert, and came to the mountain of God, even to Horeb. And the angel of the Lord appeared unto him in a flame of fire out of the midst of a bush: and he looked, and, behold, the bush burned with fire, and the bush was not consumed.

And Moses said, I will now turn aside, and see this great sight, why the bush is not burnt. And when the Lord saw that he turned aside to see, God called unto him out of the midst of the bush, and said, Moses, Moses. And he said, Here am I.

And he said, Draw not nigh hither: put off thy shoes from off thy feet, for the place whereon thou standest is holy ground. Moreover he said, I am the God of thy father, the God of Abraham, the God of Isaac, and the God of Jacob. And Moses hid his face; for he was afraid to look upon God.

And the Lord said, I have surely seen the affliction of my people which are in Egypt, and have heard their cry by reason of their taskmas-

*ters; for I know their sorrows; and I am come
down to deliver them out of the hand of the
Egyptians...Come now therefore, and I will send
thee unto Pharaoh, that thou mayest bring forth
my people the children of Israel out of Egypt*
(Exodus 3:1-8,10).

Even though God performed this supernatural
feat to get Moses' attention, Moses was still free
to choose. Had he lost all interest in God and the
supernatural? Had he forgotten the call of God?
Was the feeling of divine destiny still there?

Moses said, "I will now turn aside, and see
this great sight." He said, in effect, "Here is
something I cannot understand. Here is the supernatural. I will not ignore it or scoff at it! I will
not deny it! I will investigate it! I will turn aside
and see!"

And when the Lord saw that he turned aside,
God spoke to him and sent him forth, clothed with
signs and wonders to deliver God's people!

God calls the Church

Just as Israel, a people who had once enjoyed
the supernatural power of God, was now in Egypt,
groaning and crying to God for deliverance, so
today the church of the Lord Jesus Christ is strug-
gling to be free from the chains and shackles of
tradition. The lost need to be saved. The sick
need to be healed. The empty need to be filled.
The oppressed and possessed of the devil need to
be delivered. Time is short and the harvest is
waiting to be gathered. To do this work, the
Church needs the power of the Holy Ghost. Moses

could have done no good in Egypt without the signs and wonders. And the Church cannot do her job without "these signs and wonders that follow them that believe" (see Mark 16:17).

God has called many to deliver His people. No doubt you are a deliverer. Your life has been supernaturally spared again and again because God wants you to do His will in this challenging hour.

You have a feeling of divine destiny. You want to do more than just run around in religious circles.

Perhaps, like Moses, you have failed miserably. And, because of this, you have fled to the back side of the desert. Time has passed, and the devil has whispered, "It is too late now to ever be used of God."

Let me give you deliverers who live on the back side of the desert a word from your God— "God's gifts and His call are irrevocable—He never withdraws them once they are given."

God doesn't change His mind

God's gifts and call are irrevocable and He never withdraws them! He does not change His mind about those He calls! He knew your life from beginning to end when He called you. He knew your every mistake and sin, and He had enough faith in you to call you anyway. He has not, and will not, change His mind about it. You are responsible to carry out the call, and you will give an account for it at the judgment bar of God.

God is seeking to reach all of the deliverers by setting bushes aflame with the power and glory of God through the baptism in the Holy Ghost and fire. He is giving burning bushes to every denomination. He is giving the medical profession burning bushes. He is giving lawyers, teachers, government leaders, and ordinary people of the world their burning bushes.

Men and women in every strata of society are receiving the baptism in the Holy Ghost and fire, and they are burning bushes to their particular groups.

If you have the baptism in the Holy Ghost, you are one of these burning bushes! If you do not have the mantle of the Holy Ghost power in your life, you probably know someone who is a burning bush in your strata of society.

Will you, like Moses, turn aside to investigate these burning bushes? If you will but turn aside from your prejudice, tradition, and denominational ideas and look into this glorious outpouring of the Holy Ghost, God will speak to you, also, and send you forth, clothed with signs and wonders. You will have a ministry of deliverance. Like Moses, who went into Egypt with the Rod of God and led two million slaves to freedom, you, too, will march forth into the regions of darkness in the mighty name of Jesus and, through the power of the Holy Ghost, lead multitudes out of bondage and fear into Canaan's land of full salvation!

What are your reasons for wanting the baptism in the Holy Ghost? What are your motives? Do you have a burden for a lost and dying world? Do you long to do something for suffering, sighing, dying humanity? Are you stirred to deliver this nervous, demon-oppressed, and distraught generation? If your heart cries out to magnify and please Jesus by fulfilling His commission, then you have the right motives, and the Lord Jesus will surely baptize you in the Holy Ghost and send you forth to do His work.

CHAPTER 6

The Baptism in the Holy Ghost

Jesus said in Acts 1:5, *For John truly baptized with water; but ye shall be baptized with the Holy Ghost not many days hence.*

Jesus called this experience a "baptism." If you will keep the word "baptism" clearly fixed in your mind, you will understand what Jesus meant.

In any baptism, three elements must be present—a baptizer, a candidate, and an element in which to baptize. In water baptism, your minister is the baptizer, you are the candidate, and water is the element.

In the baptism in the Holy Ghost, Jesus is the Baptizer, you are the candidate, and the element is the Holy Ghost. When you are baptized in the Holy Ghost, Jesus does something to you. A scripture that confused me for many years was 1 Corinthians 12:13, *For by one Spirit are we all baptized into one body, whether we be Jews or Gentiles, whether we be bond or free; and have been all made to drink into one Spirit.* I thought this scripture referred to the baptism in the Holy Ghost. You will notice the scripture includes the three necessary elements. However, in this instance, the baptizer is the Holy Ghost, we are the candidates, and the element is the body of Christ. So this is regeneration—the new birth. When a person is saved, the Holy Ghost places (or immerses) him into the body of Christ.

When we speak of the baptism in the Holy Ghost, however, we are not talking about something the Holy Ghost does to us but something Jesus does to us.

Seek to be baptized

If you want to be baptized in water, you must make yourself available to the baptizer, usually your minister. No matter how much you cry and pray and long for water baptism, you must take action. You have to go to the baptizer and request him to do the baptizing! He will probably ask some questions to examine your faith and motives. When he is convinced that you are washed in the Blood and sincerely possess the right motives, he will immerse you in water, in obedience to the Lord Jesus Christ.

Likewise, no matter how much emotion you work up in your soul about the baptism in the Holy Ghost, you must come to the Baptizer, the Lord Jesus Christ, and ask for it. Many people want the baptism, but they seek the direction of men instead of Jesus. Your preacher cannot baptize you in the Holy Ghost, but Jesus can and will! I encourage you to come to Jesus with fasting and prayer. Press on through the smog and fog of tradition, and do all you can to humbly enter into His presence. Like the blind man who cried to Jesus, lift up your voice and ask for His help. Don't listen to what other people say. When others rebuked this man, he cried all the more!

And, praise God, Jesus stopped and met his need! And He will do the same for you. But you must seek the Baptizer, if you want the baptism in the Holy Ghost. *Ye shall seek me, and find me, when ye shall search for me with all your heart* (Jeremiah 29:13).

As in the case of water baptism, when you come to the Baptizer in the Holy Ghost (the Lord Jesus), He also examines your motives. You must understand that you receiving this experience is not based on your personal goodness or holiness but on His precious blood that cleanses you from every stain. He has made you worthy to receive the baptism in the Holy Ghost.

What about motives?

Jesus, like the minister, will question your motives—Why do you want the baptism in the Holy Ghost? Do you want it just to make you feel good and to make a name for yourself...or to be a great preacher and build a great church?

Jesus said, "The Spirit of the Lord is upon Me because"—because. You see, there were specific reasons for having the Spirit. What were the reasons? Luke 4:18,19 says, *The Spirit of the Lord is upon me, because He hath anointed me to preach the gospel to the poor; he hath sent me to heal the brokenhearted, to preach deliverance to the captives, and recovering of sight to the blind, to set at liberty them that are bruised, to preach the acceptable year of the Lord.*

How do your motives measure up? Do you desire to preach the Gospel to the poor, heal the

63

brokenhearted, preach deliverance to the captives and recovering of sight to the blind? Do you want to set at liberty them that are bruised and preach the acceptable year of the Lord?

What are your reasons for wanting the baptism in the Holy Ghost? What are your motives? Do you have a burden for a lost and dying world? Do you long to do something for suffering, sighing, dying humanity? Are you stirred to deliver this nervous, demon-oppressed, and distraught generation? If your heart cries out to magnify and please Jesus by fulfilling His commission, then you have the right motives, and the Lord Jesus will surely baptize you in the Holy Ghost and send you forth to do His work.

(To learn more about how to receive the baptism in the Holy Spirit, order my book, entitled *Receive the Holy Spirit*. For more information, see the list of available books on page 93.)

Since the baptism in the Holy Ghost is God's method of clothing His people with power to destroy the works of darkness, it stands to reason that the devil would lie about it, criticize it, make fun of it, and do everything possible to hinder anyone from receiving it.

CHAPTER 7

These Things Hindered Me

The Apostle Paul exhorted the church in Galatians 5:7, *Ye did run well: who did hinder you that ye should not obey the truth?*

God gave the Promised Land to the Children of Israel, but they had to conquer every foot before they could enjoy its bounties. They didn't stop because of hindrances. They believed that it was for them and that it was worth every effort to possess that land.

God promises all of His children a land that flows with milk and honey. This promised land of rest and refreshing is the baptism in the Holy Ghost. It is a land of signs, miracles, and wonders.

Since the baptism in the Holy Ghost is God's method of clothing His people with power to destroy the works of darkness, it stands to reason that the devil would lie about it, criticize it, make fun of it, and do everything possible to hinder anyone from receiving it.

I found this to be true in my life. When I visited groups who believed in the baptism in the Holy Ghost, I was greatly distracted and upset over all the noise they made. They said they were praising God, but I couldn't see what possible reason there was for all the commotion. It was a stumbling block to my denominational mind. I reasoned that God was not deaf, so why shout?

Praise with your voice

Later, I realized that God is not nervous either! He enjoys the praises of His people! The psalmist said, *Praise him upon the loud cymbals: praise him upon the high sounding cymbals. Let every thing that hath breath praise the Lord. Praise ye the Lord* (Psalm 150:5,6).

Psalm 145:1-3 says, *I will extol thee, my God, O king; and I will bless thy name for ever and ever. Every day will I bless thee; and I will praise thy name for ever and ever. Great is the Lord, and greatly to be praised; and his greatness is unsearchable.*

Psalm 22:3 says, *But thou art holy, O thou that inhabitest the praises of Israel.*

And the Levites, of the children of the Kohathites, and of the children of the Korhites, stood up to praise the Lord God of Israel with a loud voice on high (2 Chronicles 20:19).

Concerning the early Christians, the Bible said, *They lifted up their voice to God with one accord* (Acts 4:24). They were all praying at the same time!

All we denominational people plan to rejoice exceedingly and praise God with all our hearts when we get to heaven. But we don't have to wait until then! When heaven comes to us in the baptism in the Holy Ghost we will begin to praise God here!

Praise with your hands

The raising of hands in the air was another hindrance to this Baptist preacher. I tried it once.

I looked over and saw my hand in the air and it looked big and conspicuous enough to be a shovel! I felt ashamed to lift my hands in the air and it bothered me to see others do so.

The upraised hand is the universal sign of surrender! Pride is what makes us ashamed to lift our hands! When we lay aside our pride and surrender to God, we will do as Paul commanded, *I will therefore that men pray everywhere, lifting up holy hands, without wrath and doubting* (1 Timothy 2:8).

If your hands are washed in the blood of Jesus and you have no wrath, unforgiveness, bitterness of spirit, or doubt, then you will want to lift your hands to God and worship Him!

It also hindered me when people clapped their hands. But I found out that God commanded, *O, clap your hands ALL ye people* (Psalm 47:1).

It was of great concern to me that I might have to change my church and denomination if I received this experience called the baptism in the Holy Ghost. I was happy to learn that God was not the God of just one chosen denomination but the God of all flesh. God loves all of His children, no matter what their denominational affiliation. His promises are not for a certain denomination but for all. *For the promise is unto you, and to your children, and to all that are afar off, even as many as the Lord our God shall call* (Acts 2:39). This scripture indicates that Pentecost is not a denomination but an experience from God for everyone.

These and many other things hindered me.

The devil will throw every stumbling block possible into the pathway of those who are marching toward God, determined to have His power. Your determination and hunger must be so great that you refuse to be hindered by "these things." Your desire must be so intense that you will not be deterred!

Keep your eyes on the Word of God and enter into the promised land!

Many who talk of receiving the Spirit of their Master, the Lord Jesus, act as though it is the easiest thing in the world. Many who say they want the baptism in the Holy Ghost act the same way. They are willing to receive it if they can get it in a hurry.

They are busy people and cannot be bothered too much. If they can trot down an aisle and have some evangelist lay hands on them and get it over with quickly, they won't mind.

But there's no time for this talk of repentance, restitution, and forgiveness! No time to speak of sanctifying one's self wholly to God. No time to talk about power to reach a lost world!

CHAPTER 8

Thou Hast Asked a Hard Thing

And it came to pass, when the Lord would take up Elijah into heaven by a whirlwind, that Elijah went with Elisha from Gilgal. And Elijah said unto Elisha, Tarry here, I pray thee; for the Lord hath sent me to Bethel. And Elisha said unto him, As the Lord liveth, and as thy soul liveth, I will not leave thee. So they went down to Bethel.

And the sons of the prophets that were at Bethel came forth to Elisha, and said unto him, Knowest thou that the Lord will take away thy master from thy head to day? And he said, Yea, I know it; hold ye your peace. And Elijah said unto him, Elisha, tarry here, I pray thee; for the Lord hath sent me to Jericho. And he said, As the Lord liveth, and as thy soul liveth, I will not leave thee. So they came to Jericho.

And the sons of the prophets that were at Jericho came to Elisha, and said unto him, Knowest thou that the Lord will take away thy master from thy head to day? And he answered, Yea, I know it: hold ye your peace. And Elijah said unto him, Tarry, I pray thee, here; for the Lord hath sent me to Jordan. And he said, As the Lord liveth, and as thy soul liveth, I will not leave thee. And they two went on. And fifty men of the sons of the prophets went, and stood to view afar off: and they two stood by Jordan.

And Elijah took his mantle, and wrapped it together, and smote the waters, and they were divided hither and thither, so that they two went over on dry ground. And it came to pass, when they were gone over, that Elijah said unto Elisha, Ask what I shall do for thee, before I be taken away from thee. And Elisha said, I pray thee, let a double portion of thy spirit be upon me.

And he said, Thou hast asked a hard thing: nevertheless, if thou see me when I am taken from thee, it shall be so unto thee; but if not, it shall not be so (2 Kings 2:1-10).

Double-portion power

Elisha was thrilled with the supernatural, miracle-working power which Elijah possessed. His desire was to have a double portion of that power. And he received this double portion. He was so saturated with the power of God that the dead who were laid on his bones rose to life again.

And it came to pass, as they were burying a man, that, behold, they spied a band of men; and they cast the man into the sepulchre of Elisha: and when the man was let down, and touched the bones of Elisha, he revived, and stood up on his feet (2 Kings 13:21).

When Elisha asked for a double portion of the spirit of his master, Elijah did not tell him that it would be easy to receive. He did not say nonchalantly, "If that is all you want, we have no problem. Anyone can receive that. That is the easiest thing in the world to attain." He said, "Thou hast asked a hard thing."

Many who talk of receiving the Spirit of their Master, the Lord Jesus, act as though it is the easiest thing in the world. Many who say they want the baptism in the Holy Ghost act the same way. They are willing to receive it if they can get it in a hurry.

They are busy people and cannot be bothered too much. If they can trot down an aisle and have some evangelist lay his hands on them and get it over with quickly, they won't mind. But there's no time for this talk of repentance, restitution, and forgiveness. No time to speak of sanctifying one's self wholly to God. No time to talk about power to reach a lost world.

After all, this is an easy thing. It requires no concern and calls for no burden. Just come quickly and get it over with!

Elijah said, "Thou hast asked a hard thing."

So he departed thence, and found Elisha the son of Shaphat, who was plowing with twelve yoke of oxen before him, and he with the twelfth: and Elijah passed by him, and cast his mantle upon him. And he left the oxen, and ran after Elijah, and said, Let me, I pray thee, kiss my father and my mother, and then I will follow thee. And he said unto him, Go back again: for what have I done to thee? And he returned back from him, and took a yoke of oxen, and slew them, and boiled their flesh with the instruments of the oxen, and gave unto the people, and they did eat. Then he arose, and went after Elijah, and ministered unto him (1 Kings 19:19-21).

Elisha paid the price

It was a hard thing for Elisha to leave his business, but he did! It was a hard thing for him to burn his bridges behind him, but he did! He cooked one yoke of oxen with the instruments and gave a feast. He didn't say, "Go put the instruments and the oxen away. This might not work out and I may need them." No! He burned the instruments and served the oxen!

It was a hard thing for Elisha to bid his friends and family farewell, but he did! It was a hard thing for him to go to Bethel, Jericho, and on to Jordan when he was discouraged from doing so at every turn of the road, but he did!

It was a hard thing for him to keep his eyes on his master as he was taken from him in a chariot of fire and a whirlwind. He could have become more interested in the noise of the whirlwind and the supernatural visitation of the heavenly chariot than in his master, but he didn't.

It was a hard thing to pick up the mantle of Elijah and march over to the river in front of the shallow sons of the prophets who "viewed afar off." What if the mantle did no good? What if the river did not part? What if he were embarrassed? It was a hard thing to stand before them all with nothing but the word of his master, but he did!

When he cried, "Where is the Lord God of Elijah?" the waters parted. The sons of the prophets shouted, *The spirit of Elijah doth rest on Elisha* (see 2 Kings 2:14,15).

You, too, have watched your Master and been

thrilled with the supernatural. You have watched Him open the eyes of the blind, make the dumb to speak, and cause the crippled to walk. You want that power. Your cry is, "Lord, let a double portion of Your Spirit rest upon me!"

You have asked a hard thing!

You have to be empty before you can be filled, and it is hard to empty yourself of self, pride, ambition, and ulterior motives. You must be cleansed because the Lord will not put His Spirit into an unclean vessel.

It is hard to admit that you are wrong and go back and make restitution. It is hard to ask someone to forgive you. It is hard to forgive someone who has wronged you. It is painful to let the searching eyes of God locate every hidden sin and bring it out for you to face and put under the Blood.

It is hard to put Jesus before mother, father, husband, wife, son, or daughter. But Jesus said, "He that is not willing to forsake all cannot be my disciple" (see Luke 14:33).

It is hard to go to Bethel and, in deep sincerity, renew your vows. It is hard to go to Jericho where the fanatics are shouting and marching around the city. Surely there is an easier way to have the power of God than by getting mixed up with that crowd—those who shout, march, pray for the sick, cast out devils, and believe in the supernatural. It is hard to go on to Jordan, the river of death, for we love our lives so very much.

Thou hast asked a hard thing! For it is diffi-

77

cult to wade through nineteen hundred years of tradition. It is hard to go on after the power in spite of misunderstandings, relatives, and hindrances.

There are those like Ananias and Sapphira who "keep back a part of the price" and die failures. But there are those like Elisha who will pay the price! These people do not care how hard it is or what it will cost. They know the world is dying and time is flying. Someone must reach them with the power of God. These desperate people wrap their fingers in the garments of God and cry, "I will not go until You bless me!"

Those on the sidelines who view from afar off are forced to confess, "The Spirit of the Lord doth rest upon them."

Don't just sit inside the door and revel in an experience. The fields are white unto harvest and the laborers are few. The field is the world and you are anointed for the purpose of reaching that world.

Happy is the man, when his Lord doth come, shall find him so doing.

CHAPTER 9

Doorway to the Supernatural

There remaineth yet very much land to be possessed (Joshua 13:1).

The baptism in the Holy Ghost is not a goal but a doorway to the supernatural power of God.

Many have received this enduement of power and then sat down as though they had accomplished all that God had planned for them to do. They need to realize that power is for a purpose!

When I began to seek God for the ministry that the early disciples had, He baptized me in the Holy Ghost. When I walked through this door, I could see a million miles of glory and supernatural power. It was up to me to march forth and claim it. God said, *Every place that the sole of your foot shall tread upon, that have I given unto you* (Joshua 1:3).

Power for a purpose

You were saved and filled with the Spirit so that this generation might be brought to God through signs and wonders. *Behold, I and the children whom the Lord hath given me are for signs and for wonders in Israel from the Lord of hosts, which dwelleth in mount Zion. And when they shall say unto you, Seek unto them that have familiar spirits, and unto wizards that peep, and that mutter: should not a people seek unto their God?* (Isaiah 8:18,19).

Every human being came from the hands of a supernatural God. The desire for the miraculous is written within mankind. Man craves a miracle! The love of the miraculous is not a work of ignorance, but rather reveals man's intense desire to reach the unseen God.

Unless man is scripturally guided, he will go astray in his search for satisfaction. Every generation will have those who go to wizards that peep and mutter. Many will seek those with familiar spirits in their search for the supernatural. There is an abundance of false doctrines, cults, and strange religions of all kinds today, because man is seeking for more than he finds in formal religion.

God's children are made for signs and wonders. They are to be lights to seeking souls. Christians are made to sparkle with the miraculous and supernatural so those who are looking for something more may "seek unto their God".

The baptism in the Holy Ghost is the doorway to this supernatural power. Jesus said, *He that believeth on me, the works that I do shall he do also; and greater works than these shall he do; because I go unto my Father* (John 14:12). He said in Mark 16:17,18, *These signs shall follow them that believe; In my name shall they cast out devils; they shall speak with new tongues; they shall take up serpents; and if they drink any deadly thing, it shall not hurt them; they shall lay hands on the sick, and they shall recover.*

Spiritual gifts

The baptism in the Holy Ghost is to enable

82

you to fulfill these scriptures. God said through the Apostle Paul, *Now concerning spiritual gifts, brethren, I would not have you ignorant* (1 Corinthians 12:1). Many who have the baptism in the Holy Ghost know nothing of these spiritual gifts.

Paul lists these spiritual gifts, *For to one is given by the Spirit the word of wisdom; to another the word of knowledge by the same Spirit; to another faith by the same Spirit; to another the gifts of healing by the same Spirit; to another the working of miracles; to another prophecy, to another discerning of spirits; to another divers kinds of tongues; to another the interpretation of tongues* (1 Corinthians 12:8-10).

The early disciples marched forth with these supernatural gifts of the Spirit in their lives and brought multitudes to the Lord Jesus Christ. When they began to speak in tongues, three thousand lost souls found Jesus Christ as Savior (see Acts 2:41).

It was the gifts of the Spirit that enabled Peter to say to the crippled man, *Silver and gold have I none; but such as I have give I thee: In the name of Jesus Christ of Nazareth rise up and walk* (Acts 3:6). As a result, five thousand more came to the Lord (see Acts 4:4).

It was the gifts of the Spirit that empowered the apostles to perform signs and wonders among the people. *And believers were the more added to the Lord, multitudes both of men and women* (see Acts 5:12-14).

It was the gifts of the Spirit in operation that enabled Philip to bring deliverance and great joy to the city of Samaria. *And the people with one accord gave heed unto those things which Philip spake, hearing and seeing the miracles which he did. For unclean spirits, crying with loud voice, came out of many that were possessed with them: and many taken with palsies, and that were lame, were healed* (Acts 8:6,7).

It was the gifts of the Spirit that enabled Peter to bring healing to Aeneas and compel all who dwelt at Lydda and Saron to turn to the Lord (see Acts 9:34,35). Through these gifts he raised Dorcas from the dead and *many believed in the Lord* (see Acts 9:36-42).

The baptism in the Holy Ghost is the doorway to these supernatural gifts of the Spirit. And it is for everyone. No one is left out! You are to *desire spiritual gifts* (1 Corinthians 14:1). *The manifestation of the Spirit is given to every man* (1 Corinthians 12:7). The Spirit divided these gifts *to every man severally as he will* (see 1 Corinthians 12:11). If you are a believer, you should do the works of Jesus (see John 14:12). Signs should follow you (see Mark 16:17). You are to, *Neglect not the gift that is in thee* (1 Timothy 4:14). His command is to *stir up the gift of God, which is in thee* (2 Timothy 1:6).

Jesus said, *Go ye into all the world, and preach the gospel* (Mark 16:15). The world is waiting. Lost souls are at stake. We must obey the command of Jesus to reach them. This is the purpose of the power of the Holy Ghost. Go preach the Gospel—it is the power of God (see

Romans 1:16). The Holy Spirit will work if we will go. Jesus will confirm His Word.

Don't just sit inside the door and revel in "an experience." The fields are white unto harvest and the laborers are few. The field is the world and you are anointed for the purpose of reaching that world.

"Happy is the man, when his lord doth come, shall find him so doing" (see Matthew 24:46).

As for me, I have been stirred! I have been moved! I know these are serious days! I will not be deterred! I will not be denied! No weight shall cling to me! If all others fail, I will not fail! I will become the man God wants me to be!

I believe I have spoken the cry of your heart, also. I believe you and I both shall hear the Master say, "Well done, thou good and faithful servant."

CHAPTER 10

The Man You Could Have Been

But Gehazi, the servant of Elisha the man of
God, said, Behold, my master hath spared Naaman this Syrian, in not receiving at his hands that
which he brought: but, as the Lord liveth, I will
run after him, and take somewhat of him. So
Gehazi followed after Naaman. And when Naaman
saw him running after him, he lighted down from
the chariot to meet him, and said, Is all well?

And he said, All is well. My master hath sent
me, saying, Behold, even now there be come to me
from mount Ephraim two young men of the sons
of the prophets: give them, I pray thee, a talent of
silver, and two changes of garments. And Naaman
said, Be content, take two talents. And he urged
him, and bound two talents of silver in two bags,
with two changes of garments, and laid them upon
two of his servants; and they bare them before
him.

And when he came to the tower, he took them
from their hand, and bestowed them in the house:
and he let the men go, and they departed. But he
went in, and stood before his master. And Elisha
said unto him, Whence comest thou, Gehazi? And
he said, Thy servant went no whither.

And he said unto him, Went not mine heart
with thee, when the man turned again from his
chariot to meet thee? Is it a time to receive

*money, and to receive garments, and oliveyards,
and vineyards, and sheep, and oxen, and menservants, and maidservants? The leprosy therefore
of Naaman shall cleave unto thee, and unto thy
seed for ever. And he went out from his presence
a leper as white as snow* (2 Kings 5:20-27).

Elijah—a mighty prophet of God

Elijah looked about him for one to minister
to him and carry on the work after he left the
scene of battle. God led him to choose Elisha.
When Elijah was to be taken away, he asked Elisha
what his desires were. Elisha answered, *Let a
double portion of thy spirit be upon me* (2 Kings
2:9). He received that double portion and went
forth to do a mighty work for God.

Now it was Elisha's time to choose a young
man to minister to him and eventually carry on
the work. He chose Gehazi.

The record does not contain this, but it could
have. "And behold, Elisha's time of departing
came, and he called his servant Gehazi unto him
and asked, 'What do you wish before I am taken?'
Gehazi, his servant, says, 'O master, let a triple
portion of thy spirit rest upon me.' And are not
the mighty works of Gehazi recorded? Did he not
turn Israel into a right path and bring glory to the
Lord all his days?"

The record could have said that, but it didn't.
The record says that Gehazi, instead, was rotting
away with leprosy because of his own selfish desires. How he must have wept when he stood

before the Lord and saw "the man he could have been."

Think of the great and mighty ministries of today. What if they had been content to do less than their best, accumulate a little security, enhance their denominational prestige, and rest on flowery beds of ease? How would they feel, as they stand before the Lord, to see the thousands of people who could have been saved, healed, and delivered, and the nations that could have been shaken, if they had only preached the Gospel of Jesus Christ like they should have? What if they had not answered the call of God?

How startled and overwhelmed you will be when you stand before Jesus and see "the man you could have been."

And God shall wipe away all tears from their eyes (Revelation 7:17). Many of you will shed those tears when you see what you could have done to reach this lost and dying world. You will weep because you didn't fast, pray, believe, go and obey.

Gehazi failed for two reasons. He failed to be moved by the seriousness of his day. Elisha revealed this when he said to Gehazi, *Is it a time to receive money, and to receive garments, and oliveyards, and vineyards, and sheep, and oxen, and menservants, and maidservants?* (2 Kings 5:26). Gehazi's mind was not serious about the cause of the Lord. His heart was filled with thoughts of money, garments, property, and servants. He felt he had better make it while he could.

A time for action

Paul said, *And that, knowing the time, that now it is high time to awake out of sleep* (Romans 13:11). Mordecai said to Esther, *Who knoweth whether thou art come to the kingdom for such a time as this?* (Esther 4:14). This is the time to be serious about the things of God. This is a time for action.

Woe to all who, in this serious day when the souls of millions hang in the balance, get caught up with nothing more than money, garments, property, and servants for personal and selfish use! They shall surely miss God's best!

Secondly, Gehazi failed because, even though he lived in the midst of a great supernatural move, he was not concerned about seeking it for his own life. He was there when the waters of the Jordan rolled back! He was there when the bad waters were healed! He was there when God wrought a miracle and sent water in abundance without rain or cloud! He was there when the Shunamite's son was raised from the dead and when Naaman was healed of leprosy! None of this moved him. It did not thrill him. It left no lasting impression upon him. He was too busy making plans for money, garments, property and servants. His loss was great.

No generation has been as blessed as ours. God has visited us with one of the greatest supernatural moves of the Spirit in all of history. He has given us mighty ministries to stir our generation and shake nations by supernatural signs and wonders.

Will you stay so engrossed in your money-making, garments, property, and servants that you will not allow yourself to be moved to seek God and His supernatural power for yourself?

If so, your loss will be inexpressibly great!

As for me, I have been stirred! I have been moved! I know these are serious days! I will not be deterred! I will not be denied! No weight shall cling to me! If all others fail, I will not fail! I will become the man God wants me to be.

I believe I have spoken the cry of your heart, also. I believe you and I both shall hear the Master say, *Well done, thou good and faithful servant* (Matthew 25:21).

BOOKS BY JOHN OSTEEN

*A Miracle For Your Marriage
*A Place Called There
*ABC's of Faith
*Believing God For Your Loved Ones
 Deception! Recognizing True and False Ministries
 Four Principles in Receiving From God
*Healed of Cancer by Dodie Osteen
*How To Claim the Benefits of the Will
*How To Demonstrate Satan's Defeat
 How To Flow in the Super Supernatural
 How To Minister Healing to the Sick
*How To Receive Life Eternal
 How To Release the Power of God
 Keep What God Gives
*Love & Marriage
 Overcoming Hindrances To Receiving the Baptism in the Holy Spirit
*Overcoming Opposition: How To Succeed in Doing the Will of God
      by Lisa Comes
*Pulling Down Strongholds
*Receive the Holy Spirit
 Reigning in Life as a King
 Rivers of Living Water
 Saturday's Coming
 Seven Facts About Prevailing Prayer
 Seven Qualities of a Man of Faith
*Six Lies the Devil Uses To Destroy Marriages by Lisa Comes
 Spiritual Food For Victorious Living
*The Believer's #1 Need
 The Bible Way to Spiritual Power
 The Confessions of a Baptist Preacher
*The Divine Flow
*The 6th Sense...Faith
 The Truth Shall Set You Free
*There Is a Miracle in Your Mouth
 This Awakening Generation
 Unraveling the Mystery of the Blood Covenant
*What To Do When Nothing Seems To Work
*What To Do When the Tempter Comes
 You Can Change Your Destiny

*Also available in Spanish.

Please write for a complete list of prices in the John Osteen Library.
Lakewood Church • P.O. Box 23297 • Houston, Texas 77228

281-9458
Linda